by Karl Shapiro

ADULT
BOOKSTORE

ADULT BOOKSTORE

Karl Shapiro

Random House
New York

LIBRARY OF CONGRESS CATALOGING IN PUBLICATION DATA
Shapiro, Karl Jay, 1913–
    Adult bookstore.

    Poems.
    I. Title
PS3537.H27A67   811'.5'2   75–40550
ISBN 0–394–40249–9

MANUFACTURED IN THE UNITED STATES OF AMERICA

98765432

FIRST EDITION

"The Humanities Building" originally appeared in *The New Yorker*. "Girls Working in Banks," "Jefferson's Greeting," "Sestina: of the Militant Vocabulary" and "The White Negress" were first published in *Esquire Magazine*. "Moon-Walk," "Garage Sale," "A Curiosity" and "The Garage Fool" first appeared in *Audience*. "Flying First Class" and "A Parliament of Poets" were originally published in *New Republic*. "Moving In" and "The Rape of Philomel" (entitled "Philomel, Procne, Tereus") first appeared in *Poetry*. "Over Many Seas" was originally published in *California Quarterly*. "The Piano Tuner's Wife" first appeared in *Kayak*. "Adult Bookstore" first appeared in *Poetry Now*. "The Heiligenstadt Testament" was originally published in *The New York Quarterly*.

for Teri

Contents

ADULT
BOOKSTORE

• A Parliament of Poets

Two hundred poets are sitting side by side
In the government auditorium,
Waiting their turn to mount the stage
And read five minutes' worth of poems,
And then sit down again, still side by side,
The young, the old, the crazy, the sane
In alphabetical order.
Some rant their lines, some plead and some intone,
Some bellow and some simply talk.

Outside along the curb there waits a line
Of blue government buses
To carry the poets to the White House to shake hands
With the young President. The President
Is interested in shaking hands with the poets
And possibly saying something to each.

But when the alphabet has run its course
The chairman takes the lectern to announce
That the trip to the White House is called off,
The visit has been postponed
Or canceled for an indefinite period.

It appears that the President has chosen this hour
To warn the nation that a fleet of freighters,
Carrying atomic warheads on their decks
Visibly, are moving towards the coast of Cuba,
And that the President has ordered our fleet
To intercept and blockade the invaders.

And the parliament of poets disintegrates,
Some going to their hotel rooms to pack,
Some to the dark bars, some to the streets
To gaze up at the vacant Washington sky.

• The Humanities Building

All the bad Bauhaus comes to a head
In this gray slab, this domino, this plinth
Standing among the olives or the old oak trees,
As the case may be, and whatever the clime.
No bells, no murals, no gargoyles,
But rearing like a fort with slits of eyes
Suspicious in the aggregate, its tons
Of concrete, glaciers of no known color,
Gaze down upon us. Saint Thomas More,
Behold the Humanities Building!
                              On the top floor
Are one and a half professors of Greek,
Kicked upstairs but with the better view,
And two philosophers, and assorted Slavics;
Then stacks of languages coming down,
Mainly the mother tongue and its dissident children
(History has a building all its own)
To the bottom level with its secretaries,
Advisors, blue-green photographic light
Of many precious copying machines
Which only the girls are allowed to operate.
And all is bathed in the cool fluorescence
From top to bottom, justly distributed

. . . .

Light, Innovation, Progress, Equity;
Though in my cell I hope and pray
Not to be confronted by
A student with a gun or a nervous breakdown,
Or a girl who closes the door as she comes in.

The Old Guard sits in judgment and wears ties,
Eying the New in proletarian drag,
Where the Assistant with one lowered eyelid
Plots against Tenure, dreaming of getting it;

And in the lobby, under the bulletin boards,
The Baudelairean forest of posters
For Transcendental Meditation, Audubon Group,
"The Hunchback of Notre Dame," Scientology,
Arab Students Co-op, "Case of the Curious Bride,"
Two students munch upon a single sandwich.

• Flying First Class

Between the first martini and the wine
A thousand flying-miles
Over the Nevada Flats or Great Salt Lake
Or only a dirty tablecloth of sky,
A navigational turn, the wormy clouds above;
Soon it will be time to dine,
With the clocks wrong among the well-set smiles
Of stewardesses leisurely and ripe.
In first class you can smoke your English pipe.

A gilded drawing of the astrolabe
Brightens the wall of the latrine,
Making me think of that Arabian sage
And Chaucer of a greener age.

The stethoscope pumps music in my ears,
And now they drop a movie screen.

The aluminum wing, the plastic seats, the roar,
The well-dressed heads, perhaps the really rich,
All of us in the friendly arms of kitsch,
Billows of passion—a thunderhead below!
Beef Teriyaki, Caesar Salad Bowl,
Coursing the aureole,
We dream, we worry and we itch.

I see her carving meat across the aisle:
"How do you like your Château?"
Pouring French wine that looks to be
A famous label.

I settle down behind my let-down table
And get three slices of the pink Château,
Wishing I wouldn't think of that Chateaubriand
Whose Atala poisoned herself
For faith, not love,
On the Mississippi where it glints below
Between twin cities of oil and grime;
Better to drift, better to thumb your *Time*.

Fiesta Fruit Plate, coffee, B & B,
Arching from San Francisco to the utmost coasts
In variably empty sky,
Hung there invisibly
For banal destinations on the earth
Saturated with all the modern wrongs,
Mal du siècle, the sickness of the age
That God and man and history have wrought.

"Be careful," says the stewardess, "it's hot!"
Handing the small hot towels out on tongs.

• Adult Bookstore

Round the green fountain thick with women
Abstract in the concrete, water trickling
Between their breasts, wetting their waists
Girdled with wheat, pooling in the basin,
The walker pauses, shrugs, peregrinates
To the intersection, section of the city
Where forgotten fountains struggle for existence,
Shops have declined to secondhand
And marginal cultures collect like algae.
Dubious enterprises flourish here,
The massage parlor, the adult bookstore.

Their windows are either yellowed or blacked
Or whited or redded out,
Bold lettering proclaiming No Minors Allowed,
Bachelor Books, Adult Films and Cartoons.

The doorway jogs to the right at a strict angle
And everything from the street is invisible,
Keeping the law and clutching the illusion.
Inside, the light is cold and clean and bright,
Everything sanitary, wrapped in cellophane

• • • •

Which flashes messages from wall to wall
Of certain interest to the eye that reads
Or does not read: Randy, Coit,
Sex Hold-Up, Discipline, Ghetto Male,
Images of cruelty, ideas for the meek,
Scholarly peeks at French, English and Greek,
And everywhere the more than naked nude
Mystery called the wound that never heals.

Or there a surgical cabinet all glass:
Pink plastic phalli, prickly artifact,
Enlarger finger-small or stallion-size,
Inflatable love partner, five feet four,
Lotions, Hot Melt, super-double-dong,
Battery dildo (origin obscure),
Awakeners of the tired heart's desire
When love goes wrong.

The expense of spirit in a waste of shame
Is sold forever to the single stag
Who takes it home in a brown paper bag.

• Girls Working in Banks

Girls working in banks wear bouffant hair and shed
In their passage over the rather magnificent floors
Tiny shreds of perforated paper, like body flakes.
They walk through rows of youngish vice-presidents
With faraway looks, who dandle pencils and tend to ignore
The little tigerish lights flashing on their telephones.
When the girls return to their stations behind a friendly grid
They give out money neatly or graciously take it,
For not far from them the great interior glow of a vault
Built out of beaten dimes, stands open, shines,
Beaming security without ostentation.
If you glance inside it, there's nothing to be seen
But burnished drawers and polished steel elbows
Of the great machine of the door. It's a speckless world
With nobody inside it, like the best room in the gallery
Awaiting the picture which is still in a crate.
The girls change places frequently, moving their own addresses
From Open to Closed, Next Counter, or they walk away
With surprising freedom behind a wall or rise up on escalators
Past aging and well-groomed guards whose pistols seem
Almost apologetic as they watch people
Bending over Formica stand-up desks writing
With ballpoint pens attached to rosary chains,

•   •   •   •

After which the people select a queue in which they stand
Pious, abashed at the papery transactions,
And eventually walk with the subtlest sense of relief
Out of revolving doors into the glorious anonymous streets.

• Crossing Lincoln Park

Dit le corbeau, jamais plus. —Mallarmé

Car locked, I started home across the grass,
A kind of island with a stand of oaks
Washed round on all sides by the swish of cars,
To where I lived, a hundred yards in view.
Quarried apartments rose on every hand,
Scoriac Gothic shouldering solid glass
Hemming me in, reflecting a blank sky.
Briefcase and I happily homeward strode
Through ankle-grass, when something at my shoe
Darkly turned over, what I never knew,
For down came the crow and with a sudden blow,
Its great wings beating, slashed at my face
With croak and scream and yellow beak
Screeching me out. I did not stop to think
But leapt and sprinted toward the curb, the bird
Cursing, crisscrossing, driving at my face,
Crashing my shoulders with its filthy wings.
Ugly, omnivorous offal-eating crow,
Bird of ill omen,
Eater of turd and dead fish, get thy beak
From out my heart! My eyeglasses flew off,
I stumbled forward, clutching my briefcase,
Fanning away the bird with naked hand,

•   •   •   •

Until I reached the street where solid cars
Bumper to bumper blocked my flight,
And still the crow surrounded me and struck
Till I broke through and in the door and up
The elevator to the velvet hall
And to the door and in, where your bright smile
Changed instantly to—"White!" you said.
"Your face whiter than chalk!"

• The White Negress

(Brancusi—Chicago Art Institute)

Who has not seen Brancusi's White Negress?
O quarryman who cut her from the mountain,
Did you see her breathing in the mountain?
Geology, what did you have in mind!

Slightly smaller than life, her head
Stands up like a magnolia bud
In snowy marble,
With a little marble ribbon tying her hair in the back,
Matching her slightly spread nose
And her pretty protruding lips,
The White Negress in all her marble beauty,
So black, so white!

• Jefferson's Greeting

At the foot of his mountain he stops the carriage
For the first glimpse of the white Palladian dome
That tops his house; then up the bluish hills
Of Albemarle, past garden and vine,
When suddenly there burst from every side
The blacks, who pull the horses from the shafts
And haul him like a chariot up the drive,
Cheering, dancing, crying his return,
Lifting the master bodily
Up the steps and over the threshold,
Kissing his hands and feet, even the ground
He passes over, the great Virginian home,
Whose wilderness he carved into decorum.

• My Father's Funeral

Lurching from gloomy limousines we slip
On the warm baby-blanket of Baltimore snow,
Wet flakes smacking our faces like distraught
Kisses on cheeks, and step upon the green
Carpet of artificial grass which crunches
Underfoot, as if it were eating, and come
To the canopy, a half-shelter which provides
A kind of room to enclose us all, and the hole,
And the camp chairs, and following after,
The scrolly walnut coffin
That has my father in it.

Minutes ago in the noncommittal chapel
I saw his face, not looking himself at all
In that compartment hinged to open and shut,
A vaudeville prop with a small waxen man,
"So cold," the widow said and shied away
In a wide arc of centrifugal motion,
To come again to stand like me beside,
In the flowerless room with electric candelabra.
If there is among our people any heaven,
We are rather ambiguous about it
And tend to ignore the subject.

The rabbi's eulogy is succinct,
Accurate and sincere, and the great prayer
That finishes the speech is simply praise
Of God, the god my father took in stride
When he made us learn Hebrew and shorthand,
Taught us to be superior, as befits
A nation of individual priests.
At my sister's house we neither pray nor cry
Nor sit, but stand and drink and joke,
So that one of the youngsters says
It's more like a cocktail party.

For Dylan's dandy villanelle,
For Sylvia's oath of damnation one reserves
A technical respect. To Miller's Willie
And Lewis's Babbitt I demur.
My father was writing a book on salesmanship
While he was dying; it was his book of poems,
Destined to be unpublished. He hadn't time
To master books but kept the house well stocked
With random volumes, like a ship's library,
Rows and rows of forgotten classics,
Books for the sake of having books.

My father in black knee-socks and high shoes
Holding a whip to whip a top upstreet;
My father the court stenographer,
My father in slouch hat in the Rockies,
My father kissing my mother,
My father kissing his secretary,
In the high-school yearbook captioned Yid,
In synagogue at six in the morning praying
Three hundred and sixty-five days for his mother's rest,
My father at my elbow on the bimah
And presiding over the Sabbath.

In the old forgotten purlieus of the city
A Jewish ghetto in its day, there lie
My father's father, mother and the rest,
Now only a ghetto lost to time,
Ungreen, unwhite, unterraced like the new
Cemetery to which my father goes.
Abaddon, the old place of destruction;
Sheol, a new-made garden of the dead
Under the snow. Shalom be to his life,
Shalom be to his death.

• The Sense of Beauty

The human form is seldom beautiful,
Less beautiful than animal in zoo.
The human mind with beauty is accursed,
Man being esthetic animal.
Man is the only beast that measures busts,
Bottoms and teeth and feet and length of bone.
Man of all living things worships the new,
Man of all creatures thinks he must be first,
Thinks he must intellectualize his lusts.
Man is the only animal alone,
And only man invents his Caliban.
The only esthetic animal is man.

Therefore a prince in cloth of paradise
Would keep a dwarf to emphasize his state;
A whore therefore, a power behind the throne,
Would lead her monkey on a gold device.
Cripples strike fear in children and in hags.
People stare into mirrors not from pride
But to decide if it is not too late
To reconstruct the esthetic of the bone.
Charles Baudelaire saw beauty in the rags
Of beggar girls; sickness he deified,
Taking to bed the abscess of the soul.
Man is an esthetic animal.

The human face most seldom is divine
But tends to beast, as nature plans its fall.
God's image, what is left of it, demands
An ignoble etching of authentic line.
The human face unlighted by its sun
Sits in the flesh and sinks in golden mud.
Man is an esthetic animal
And practices the laying-on of hands
Of clay, of sounds, of language and of stone
In imitation of the clay of God.
The human form is seldom beautiful.
Man is an esthetic animal.

The human form is seldom beautiful,
More seldom is the human face divine.
Man is an esthetic animal,
Being the only beast that yearns for style.
Toulouse at the butt-end of his career,
"At last I have forgotten how to draw!"
And then could draw the truly perfect line.
War is an esthetic principle;
The greatest poets have celebrated war.
Man is the victim of esthetic law.
Man is the esthetic animal
Whose human form is seldom beautiful.

The human form is seldom beautiful,
Less beautiful than animal in zoo.
The human mind with beauty is accursed,
Man being esthetic animal.
Man is the only beast that measures busts,
Bottoms and teeth and feet and length of bone.
Man of all living things worships the new,
Man of all creatures thinks he must be first,
Thinks he must intellectualize his lusts.
Man is the only animal alone,
And only man invents his Caliban.
The only esthetic animal is man.

· Writer in Exile

Cold and to the north of recognition,
Beyond the kingdom of letters, back-biting banquets,
Scandals, bequests, laurels and fellowships,
Should I petition the President, kowtow to the Emperor
From this wasteland of oil-pipes and guns
Where the natives wear skins, speak an unwritten tongue
And stagger drunk through sleet? Well, here I am,
Writer and poet of international reputation,
Ironist, sophisticate and wit
Dreaming of oleanders in the sculpture gardens
And fountains thundering into marble laps,
Equestrian statues of the dear Confederate dead,
The noble bronzes in the brainwashed blue.
I'm out of it with my highbrow jabs at government,
Dirty cracks about the chiefs of staff,
Steel industrialists' wives, all that canaille
Whose favorite word is Honor, the old code word
For guilty. I didn't uproot the sacred olive,
Poisoned nobody, forged no documents.
Impious perhaps? Neutral during sedition?
Adulterous? Seducing the minds of matrons?
Undermining the family and the Constitution?
Loose charges easy to concoct to stick.
I'm stuck with being too familiar with the great,
Knowing too much, seeing it all and then

Writing it down to amuse myself and tickle the world.
The world was not amused and I am banished,
Exiled or, as they call it nowadays, *relegated*.
A truck goes by, bouncing barrels of beer,
Letters are brought; someone writes that my furniture is stolen,
My house vandalized: signed A Friend. Some friend.
My books are banned from the public libraries, however
Private copies are circulated and quoted
At cabinet meetings and by Big Chairman himself.
It snows and snows and makes my fire smoke.
I'm fifty, I'm harmless, I'm good; I'll stand my ground and die;
My life was moral though my Muse was lax.
The peasants are friendly; I invite them in for a drink,
Answer their questions about famous temples,
Roads as swift as glass, the Commissar's sexual vices,
Restaurant prices, rise of the Eastern cults.
Should I write a poem for the Boss in the local dialect,
Dedicated to the Great Society,
The New Frontier, New Deal, Utopia, whatever,
Hopefully to get home to climb the marble stairs
Under the Eagle, past the Marines, into the Presence?

• The Heiligenstadt Testament

(Beethoven dying)

The first time that he opened me
with his knife like a pomegranate
I watched my brown blood spurt across the floor
I was brave I was relieved
the second time relieved
the third time I yelled
call for the priest
no more get me the priest
too late too late
the fire draws the wind
my brother Ludwig died in infancy

Note: As the Heiligenstadt Testament, the will in which Beethoven threatened suicide, is one unbroken sentence, so did I conceive of Beethoven's deathbed delirium. The data of the poem are all grounded in fact and may be traced to the *Life* by Alexander Wheelock Thayer, the biography to which all subsequent studies of Beethoven must refer. Thayer was an American. It is tempting to think that Abraham Lincoln may be credited indirectly for the great *Life*; Lincoln appointed Thayer American consul at Trieste, possibly to enable him to pursue the biography.

Beethoven the man has been mythologized as the great Romantic, revolutionary, etc. The actual Beethoven, on the contrary, was profoundly and conservatively religious, patriotic, cautious, practical and even puritanical.

I was next
and so they named me Ludwig
he was replaced
I sign my name Louis at times
my mother was a palace servant
my father a tenor at the court
and a horrible drunkard
van is not von
and passed me off as a *Wunderkind*
lying about my birth date
I was no *Wunderkind*
Beethoven the bungler
I learned to improvise so well on the organ
at eight because my fingers froze
my feet froze in the church
since fifteen I have supported
the entire family
and am the first to sit with princes
and summon kings with my baton
to the concert hall
the entire congress of crowned kings
and would have worn my medal
beloved medal of the King of France
except somebody said it would rumple my collar
so did not wear it but left it in my room

and Waldstein befriended me
van is not von
and Haydn wasn't impressed with my playing
or with me
the old man's heart breaking
for the death of Mozart
but I continued my lessons with him
and studied counterpoint in secret
was Mozart poisoned as they say
by Salieri by competition
who poisoned my ears
Waldstein and the Archduke
played the quartets admirably
at six o'clock in the morning
I keep time by the motion of their bows
that way can almost hear my music
and in some palace or other
improvise improvise yelled the fools
and I improvised for the fools
and when I turned round from the keyboard
after two hours
some of them were sobbing with ecstasy
and I stood up and faced them and yelled
you fools you fools
I exploded pianos

                    big ones little ones
            after the gilded horizontal harps
                    I needed more octaves
        the mahogany thunder was good for my ears
            and drowned out the infernal buzzing
                        deaf
                    if you are deaf
                and you are Beethoven
                    what do you do
                you sing you laugh you dance
                you sing at the top of your voice
    that was the way I scared the peasant on the road
            and his oxen bolted and they all bolted
            and I sat down and laughed and wept
        and my friends detected that I couldn't hear
            the shepherd piping close at hand
                and I saw the look in their eyes
                    and said nothing
        and back at the cottage at Heiligenstadt
                began to write my will
            you who think I am malevolent
                stubborn misanthropic
    are right because you do not know my secret
    I who all my life was the soul of gentleness
            decency and high ambition

have for six years been suffering
a permanent malady
the greatest of all imaginable curses
compelling me to loneliness
bitterness and despair
for I Beethoven am deaf I am deaf
Beethoven has no ears
how can I say to other men speak louder
raise your voice
therefore forgive me when I draw away
when I would joyfully mingle with you all
and hear the shepherd's piping or a cough
if I could hear a cough
I live in exile when I must approach
a fellow-man I am seized with horror
suppose that I Beethoven am found out
and am laughed out of the room
come death quickly come when you will
and divide my fortune
and I have no wife and my servants are bitches
that follows especially because I am deaf
how can I hear what they're stealing
yet someone has taken my filthy suit
and left a tailored new one in its place
enemy or friend

trust nobody
because I scribbled
notes on the shutter next the piano
the landlady has sold the shutters
to a curious tourist
and demands that I Beethoven
pay for new shutters
trust nobody
especially publishers
hellhounds that licked and gnawed my brains
God damn all publishers all but the English
God bless the English and the Philharmonic
God bless their national anthem
the English shamed my publishers
into paying me something
I saved my money
40,000 for Karl nobody else
thunder lightning and snow
all on my deathbed
that will make for a massive funeral
for Beethoven 20,000 at the iron gates
God bless the English they have sent me
the forty-volume edition of Handel
Handel the greatest of us all
they will sing Mozart for my mass

then Cherubini excellent
in excellent taste
and will close the schools for my funeral
and 40,000 florins all for Karl
dear nephew your mother was a whore
lewdness and irreverence two things beyond me
and when I took you from her house
you tried to blow your brains out
and almost succeeded
you don't approve my love
you steal my manuscripts and sell them
and run back to your mother the whore
I did my best to make you hate your mother
and didn't succeed but you are mine
I should have married
not Bettina Goethe's butterfly
who fluttered to me from Goethe
one of those women that collect great men
bearing the honey of genius mouth to mouth
her personal mission her errand
or my immortal beloved I forget her name
my angel my all my very self
my coach broke down in the forest
it had only four horses
Esterhazy had eight

yet I got pleasure from that
overcoming difficulties
remain my true my only treasure
I forget her name
for my Tenth I have it planned
the Goethe Faust
but the old man won't answer my letters
my Ninth I dedicated to the King of Prussia
who in turn gave me a diamond ring
and an innocent bird the yellowhammer
common in Austria as in luscious England
which I shall never see
gave me the theme of my Fifth
I altered the birdsong slightly
and made it the eagle of my pen
the same I did with the singing of peasants
my Battle Symphony my birds
where are my multiplication tables
is it true that any child can understand them
40,000 florins for Karl
let nobody say Beethoven was a fool
too late too late
the fire draws the wind
the wine has not arrived

FROM CALIFORNIA

· Moving In

I wish you for your birthday as you are,
Inherently happy,
The little girl always shining out of your face
And the woman standing her ground.

Wish you the seldom oceanic earthquake
Which shatters your gaze
Against some previous interior past
And rights you.

Wish you your honesty normal as a tree
Confounding the caws of intellectuals.
When I zip your dress I kiss you on the neck,
A talisman in honor of your pride.

When I hold your head in my hands
It is as of the roundness of Columbus
Thinking the world, "my hands capable of
Designing the earthly sphere."

Your fingers on the piano keys
Or the typewriter keys or on my face
Write identical transcriptions.
Nothing you do is lost in translation.

I am delighted that you loathe Christmas.
I feel the same way about Communism.
Let us live in the best possible house,
Selfish and true.

May the Verdi *Requiem* continue to knock you out
As it does me; fashionable protest art
Continue to infuriate your heart
And make you spill your drink.

Now ideology has had its day
Nothing is more important than your birthday.
Let us have a solid roof over our head
And bless one another.

• Moon-Walk

The night before the men walked on the moon
You took the kids to the movies in the dark.
I pondered now if soon
Women would stop their periods and tides
Lie stagnant and the waves desist.

The neighbor behind us is a scientist;
His lights were on and in between them shone
The light leaves of the eucalyptus tree
Whose barely moving tracery
Revealed the spaces of the night that hides.

How quiet are the moon-men at their tasks,
Moving through nothing awesomely.
It is an awesome time when love takes on
The consequences of the untrodden moon.
Awesome it is without you in this room.

• The Moss Roses

When wineglasses were flowers (like Tiffany tulips)
And there was stained glass in the dining room
And brown was beautiful,
One would have grown, leaned over, looked at moss roses
(Purslane, porcelaine, *Portulaca grandiflora!*)

Flowers of Art Nouveau! crawling over the slab,
Fluttering like butterflies, three-quarters dead, exotic,
Neo-decadent, succulent, opening soft, shutting at will,
Redon-Gaudí dream-flowers, musical-mystical blooms,
Colors of kleenex, texture of old letter-paper, petals
That flutter like dead moth wings, one at a time,
More than saffron, more than purple, incarnadine,
Waterless white, lustrous cerise, salmon, pastel,
Lavender, orange, pink on the hot dry banks, parking strips,
Gravel beds, patio insets, edgings, in any soil
In the sandy loam, in the terrible heat, self-sown
Low on the ground with stand-still insects sucking,
Insects tiny as smuts in the baby-face jungle,
Drawing the tiny dust-black butterflies, the purslane moths
Amidst the crawly fleshy stems, the edible,
In the Middle Ages used for salads, pickling, curing warts.

And when we pluck them from their bed they undergo
No spectacular suffering, like mandrake or rainbow trout,
But where a while ago they were so thick
We neaten up the plot with crushed red brick.

· A Curiosity

Tiny bees come to see what I am,
Lying in the sun at summer's end,
Writing a poem on a reclining chair.
A butterfly approaches and retreats;
Flies bang into my body by mistake,
And tinier things I can't identify;
And now and then a slow gigantic wasp
Rows on its stately voyage to the fence.
The trees are still too little to have birds;
Besides, the neighbors all have special cats
Bred for their oddity or arrogance.
A dragonfly sips at a lemon twig
After a helicopter landing. It
Appears that I am a curiosity
In my own backyard.
The dog of doubtful breed
Sleeps on the carpet of the sod,
And a bee necks with a rose.

• Detail

The cat eats the praying mantis
By punching it to death,
Pushing it with her paws,
Playing soccer with it,
Tossing it in the air,
Carrying it around in her jaws
And finally, when the insect
Has no more motion or flutter,
Chewing its green head off.

• Garage Sale

Two ladies sit in the spotless driveway
Casually smoking at the not-for-sale card table,
Over their heads a row of plastic pennants,
Orange, yellow, assorted reds and blues,
Such as flap over used-car lots, a symbol.
Each thing for sale is hand-marked with a label,
And every object shows its homemade bruise.

They sit there all day, sometimes getting up
When a visitor asks a question about a crib
Or a box spring with a broken rib
Or a gas jet to start fireplace fires.

Cars park gently, some with daisy decals,
No Mark IV's, Coupe de Villes or Corvettes;
Mostly wagons with the most copious interiors,
And few if any intellectuals.

All day the shoppers in low-key intensities,
Hoping to find something they are trying to remember
Fits in, or sticks out, approach and mosey,
Buy a coffee mug with a motto, or leave,
And nobody introduces him or herself by name.
That is taboo. And nobody walks fast. That is taboo.
And those who come look more or less the same.

A child buys a baby dress for her Raggedy Anns.
A pair of andirons, a mono hi-fi, a portable
              typewriter, square electric fans,
Things obsolescing but not mature enough to be
              antiques,
And of course paintings which were once expensive
Go or can go for a song.

This situation, this neighborly implosion,
As flat as the wallpaper of Matisse
Strikes one as a cultural masterpiece.
In this scene nothing serious can go wrong.

• The Martini

In Hell
Said Randall Jarrell
Americans tell each other
How to make a martini.

About the shape of the glass there is little dispute,
More about the garnish,
Whether a twist, olive, onion or nothing,
And everyone is in accord about the temperature,
Just above freezing,
And the color all but colorless.

The ritual is the thing,
Holding the stem of the chalice to the light,
Somewhat to bless the dying day.

To tell the truth,
Four drops of California Chablis
Are better than seven drops of French vermouth.

But ever you are ready to begin,
Be extra careful not to bruise the gin.

• California Petrarchan

I hear the sunset ambulances surround
Suburbia at the turquoise edge of day,
Loping along the not-too-far freeway
Where olive trees and red bloodshed abound.
The oleanders with a shore-like sound
Perform their dance beside my own driveway
As if they also had a word to say
In all their whiteness beautifully gowned.

This Italy with insanity all its own
Lacks only history to make it true
And bitterness that ripens hour by hour.
This baby Italy, more straw than stone,
Stumbling, choking, fighting toward the New,
Bursts into flame with its own fire power.

· Death of the Fig

In troublous night the wind took out the fig
With a flying tackle, with a rapist's leap,
And laid it on the ground, wrecked at the base,
Thick and silvery, unconscious and prostrate
With all its fat green foliage, fat white figs.
By morning the fat fruit begins to drop
Like surrealist raindrops, by ten o'clock
The leaves begin to scrunch and die
A very sudden and immediate death.
I walk around it like an auto wreck
Muttering goddammit and get the pruning saw
Curved like a scimitar to waste the tree.
Flies are already gathering on the fruit,
Mashed honey-bellies, honey-leaking glands.
I saw as if in a tremendous hurry,
Becoming frenzied, using a larger saw,
Rose-clippers for twigs, wearing me out.
Now there's a yellow bee, now two or three
Burrowing into the pulp, signaling me
To hold it or give them a chance, or else
(Somebody is going to have some white-fig honey).
And finally I stack the sticky wood
Leaving three feet of trunk and four branch stumps,

A mutilate, a monster upsidedown,
Four-legged cripple without head
To paint with luminous paint for Halloween
Beside the front-door pumpkin, trick or treat.

• The Piano Tuner's Wife

That note comes clear, like water running clear,
Then the next higher note, and up and up
And more and more, with now and then a chord,
The highest notes like tapping a tile with a hammer,
Now and again an arpeggio, a theme,
As if the keyboard spoke to the one key,
Saying, No interval is exactly true,
And the note whines slightly and then truly sings.

She sits on the sofa reading a book she has brought,
A ray of sunlight on her white hair.
She is here because he is blind. She drives.
It is almost a platitude to say
That she leads him from piano to piano.

And this continues for about an hour,
Building bridges from both sides of the void,
Coasting the chasms of the harmonies.

And in conclusion,
When there is no more audible dissent,
He plays his comprehensive keyboard song,
The loud proud paradigm,
The one work of art without content.

• Mature Garden

I found the bird that annoys you;
It's squeaking in the pomegranate tree
And is gray and white with a long tail.
I think it's the female
Because a bigger one of the same kind
Is coming and going to the same tree,
Bringing it food and trying to be kind.
Maybe there's a nest that I can't see.
I'm sitting here as quiet as a ghost
Waiting for you to turn into the drive,
And writing in the style of Robert Frost.

Now they've switched to the almond tree, up high,
And he is feeding her—a butterfly!

• The Garage Fool

Man's heart expands to tinker with his car
For this is Sunday morning. —MacNeice

The garage fool starts his engines on Sunday morning
About nine or ten, when sluggards are sleeping
And pious people in pews,
Beginning with his mechanical edger,
Edging his lawn to a Euclidean line,
Then yanks his power-mower to a roar,
And roars his grass and vacuums it as well.
Next comes the buzz-saw with its silvery teeth
Screaming and lopping his lumber,
And after hammering for half an hour,
Pot-shotting the sabbatical ears of rest,
Graduates to the pruning, which requires the chain-saw,
Indian war-whoops, banshee shrieks,
Groaning of greenwood, and at last silence,
A blessed gathering of boughs,
A going into the house
Where one imagines the toy pop of a beer can
And the insect clicking of a TV dial.

• My Fame's Not Feeling Well

My fame's not feeling well;
Maybe I should get it a Fulbright
To Luxembourg or Mexico,
Or maybe send it to a doctor-critic.
The doctor will say: "It should join a committee
Or win a national prize
Or judge a contest or apologize
For something, or just crawl out of its shell.
There's really nothing I can recommend."

Maybe I'll send it to Chicago where
A cabdriver once recognized it
Driving to O'Hare.

On the other hand I'd rather let it ail,
Being quite certain that it cannot fail
And simply come to an oblivious end.
Maybe it only needs a famous friend.

All the same it is slightly diabetic
And drinks more than its share of dry white wine,
But takes its dyazide and reserpine.

Sloth, acedia, ennui, otiose pride
Got it into this fix, so let it be.
I'm not the one to take its history.

Sestina: of the Militant Vocabulary

The first word you must know is *relevant*,
The qualifier of *experience.*
Relevant experience of the *revolution*,
For instance, trains you to confront the *pigs*,
The first defense line of the *power structure*,
Which guards insidiously the *Establishment*.

What we are after is the Establishment,
Which acts as if we are not relevant
And forces us to wreck the power structure.
This confrontation is an experience
Not only for the people but for the pigs
Whom we'll win over in the revolution.

When we make love we make the revolution,
As war is made by the Establishment,
For in our confrontation with the pigs
We prove to them that they're irrelevant
And immaterial to the experience,
Which in itself can wreck the power structure.

The military-industrial power structure,
A major target of the revolution,

. . . .

Must also be a sexual experience.
To expose the symbols of the Establishment
Expose yourself—it's highly relevant
And absolutely petrifies the pigs.

In our utopia there will be no pigs
And no remains of any power structure
Except what we decide is relevant;
And what is relevant but revolution?
We spell the death of the Establishment,
Which will probably welcome the experience.

Meanwhile, experience the experience;
Demand, demand, and overwhelm the pigs
Till we in fact are the Establishment
And constitute a groovy power structure.
Remember the slogan of the revolution:
Now is forever; Now is relevant.

While pigs perpetuate the power structure,
Baby, be relevant to the revolution
Till we experience the Establishment.

OVER MANY SEAS

• The Stroke and the Dot

Katushika Hiroshige   1760–1849

Since I was six I have been mad about drawing.
By the time I was fifty I had given the public
A vast number of drawings, but nothing I did
Before I was seventy was worth a jot.
By seventy-three I had come to understand
Something of the true nature of animals,
Plants, insects and fishes. It follows that
By eighty I shall have made a certain progress,
By ninety see into the mystery of things.
If I should live to be one hundred ten,
Then everything I do,
Even if it is no more upon the sheet
Than a stroke and a dot,
The stroke and the dot will be my masterpiece.

—Signed: the old man crazy about drawing.

• Eclogue: America and Japan

(July, 1853)

A. Cast off those lines!
    Nobody else permitted aboard!
    Disperse those smallboats or we open fire!
    Send out the survey company!
    This is the fleet of the United States;
    Our guns are shotted and ready;
    Small arms at hand; sentinels at post.
    We have entered the forbidden world of Japan,
    The land Columbus himself was looking for,
    Cipango he called it. For centuries now
    No man has been permitted to set foot
    In the Emperor's domain. On penalty of death
    No man can leave it or come back to die.
    Even the fisherman blown out to sea
    Must stay estranged. Strange secret laws.
    What is the secret that they have to guard?
    Last night the watchfires flared on every hill
    And great gongs boomed around the bay;
    The immediate question is whether the shore
    Will open fire or we will
    And the whole ancient secret go up in smoke.

J. The long-nosed Americans in the deep black ships
    Are carrying fire into our peaceful ports,
    Claiming an audience with the Emperor.

How can we tell them there is no Emperor
Except a bird in a cage, in a distant palace?
How can we tell them our history?
How can we rid ourselves of these barbarians
Without drawing the unreturnable sword?
Suppose they call to life an Emperor;
The Emperor of Japan will come to life.
The Emperor is a doll; they will hand him a sword
And he will destroy us.

A.   Attention! I wish to convey the compliments
Of the President of the United States.
We are a nation of free men and the newest
Of sovereign peoples, and we come in peace
To your ancient Empire to invite Japan
Into the community of modern nations.

J.   It is the courteous demand of my government
That you withdraw your vessels immediately
And dispatch a single ship to Nagasaki.
You are violating the law of centuries
In entering this Bay. If Your Excellency persists,
We cannot answer for the consequences.
It is contrary to our law for foreigners
To enter here; please to respect our law
And depart for Nagasaki, where we shall meet.

A.   I come in peace from a peaceful country
      And in the name of God, with the sole object
      Of delivering a letter to your Emperor
      From our President, if possible, in person.
J.   It is not possible; our laws forbid it.
A.   We are a peaceful nation on a peaceful mission
      But our ships are ready for emergencies.
      We are only the first wave of our ocean navy;
      The rest is on the way. The Emperor
      Must perceive our determination.
J.   Did not your country lately invade
      The nation of Mexico and seize their lands?
A.   We have paid for the Mexican lands in gold.
      But we did not steam to Japan in the spirit of war;
      We come to announce the enlightened law of man;
      We demand your hearing as a right;
      We demand the right of communication.
      Your country has imprisoned shipwrecked sailors,
      Refuses food and water to foreign ships;
      American castaways have been caged and tortured.
J.   I do not make the laws. Your Excellency
      Has a mistaken idea of our government.
      We excel all men in reverence for life.
      We alone in the entire world
      Have known true peace for three hundred years.

We know about your wars and revolutions.
We have the secret of the art of peace.
Now you will force upon a civilized people
Your law and way of life.
We are the lovers of nature and poetry.
You come pointing your black cannon.
Consider who is humane and who is not.

A.   Our single objective is to deliver a letter
From the American President to your Emperor.
We do not require an immediate answer
But will return in half a year
To accept his reply.

J.   We are not prepared to receive your message;
The letter must be delivered to the proper agents
Of the Emperor at the proper port.
The ships are moving! Stop them
Or you will be fired upon! No foreign sail
Has ever passed this promontory!

A.   We are sounding the harbor. We shall need
Good anchorage for the rest of the fleet.
The British and French and Russian fleets
Are also on the way. —Drop anchor!
Recall the survey boats!
Stand within distance of our guns!

J.   We have no choice but to receive the letter.

One law is broken, then two, then all.
I will convey the President's letter
To the Imperial Palace and render a receipt.
You cannot expect an answer for a year.

A.   A year is too long; six months is enough.
We have already concluded an agreement with China.
As have the European powers.
There is not much time for the Emperor.

J.   The Emperor is old and weak and dying;
We cannot be forced. But I will bear the letter.
Soldiers are running in every direction;
The women have taken to the hills.
The politicians of the Emperor's party
Are scurrying to the ecclesiastical city
Where the Imperial moth has been gnawing
His silken cocoon for centuries.
Will these red-faced barbarians give him wings?
The play stops and the temples fall
In a shower of gold;
The magicians run to the caves
To brood on the mystery;
The foreigners come, bigger, indifferent,
Outlandish. The invasion is already successful.

A.   The President of the United States to
His Imperial Majesty, the Emperor:

Great and good friend,
I send you this letter by my Commodore,
An officer of the very highest rank,
Commander of the squadron now visiting
Your Imperial Majesty's dominions.
I have directed him to assure Your Highness
That I have no other object in this voyage
But to propose to Your Imperial Majesty
That America and Japan should live in friendship
And have commercial intercourse
With one another. Our Constitution and laws
Forbid all interference with religion
Or political concerns of other nations.
Our nation lies directly opposite
To yours. Our steamships can go
From California to Japan in eighteen days.
Our great state of California produces
Sixty million dollars in gold per year.
We invite your settlers to our golden state.
Japan is also rich and fertile. Let us
Trade freely with one another.
We know your ancient laws forbid such trade,
But it would seem wise, from time to time,
To make new laws. Nor do we propose
A permanent agreement. An experiment

Of a few years will do. We propose
Commerce between us, protection for our whalers
And their crews; the right to buy coal.
Friendship, humanity, coal.
May the Almighty have Your Majesty
In His great and holy keeping. Therefore
We beg Your Majesty to accept these gifts
Of no great value in themselves
But tokens of our sincere friendship.

J. We beg Your Excellency to accept these gifts
From the Empire of Japan.

A. One telegraph and four bundles of telegraph wire.

J. One flower holder and stand.

A. Seventeen Hall's rifles, twenty army pistols,
Three Maynard's muskets.

J. One box branch coral and feather in silver.

A. One barrel of whiskey for the Emperor.

J. Eight boxes of dolls.

A. One camera daguerreotype. One box acid.

J. Fifty pieces of striped taffeta.

A. A quantity of cordials for the Emperor;
A number of baskets of champagne for the Emperor.

J. Four boxes of assorted sea shells.

A. One locomotive with rails.

J. Three hundred chickens.

A.   One set of standard balancers. Five zinc plates.
J.   Ten jars of soy.
A.   One box of insulators. One box of clocks.
     A telescope for the Emperor.
J.   Oak charcoal, thirty-five boxes.
A.   One box gutta-percha wires.
J.   One box flowered notepaper.
A.   Eight baskets Irish potatoes.
J.   Twenty-nine parasols.
A.   Two carbines; twelve cavalry swords.
J.   One box, thirty brooms.
A.   Ten ship's beakers containing one hundred gallons
     Of whiskey for general distribution.
     —The works of the master bird-lover Audubon.

· Death of the Yamoto

(April, 1945)

Out of the Inland Sea
Into the Eagle's claws
We sail to suicide.

Yamoto, biggest battleship ever built,
Most beautiful to commit
The biggest suicide of all.

Only the Floating Chrysanthemums remain,
Petals drifting into American flak,
To die for the Emperor.

Their ships rose up from Pearl like ghosts,
Their wings blacken the sun;
We proceed to our dying.

Yamoto they say is unsinkable,
Our sister-ship *Mushashi* was unsinkable
But heeled over and sank.

An American admiral Morrison writes of us,
Singularly beautiful ship,
A graceful sheer to her flush deck

·　·　·　·

Unbroken from stem to stern
With streamlined mast and stack,
Seventy thousand tons of steel.
Yamoto means Japan.

War is like kendo with bamboo spears,
War is like haiku for surprise;
The sudden stroke at Pearl, at Singapore,
Philippines, Malaysia,
All the way to our own great south,
But after that, no more surprises.

Yet even now the Divine Wind
That sank the ships of Genghis Khan
Might bring us peace with honor
And quench the Flowers of Edo
That burn our people in their beds.

When we had sunk *Repulse* and *Prince of Wales*
We did not strafe the watery survivors,
Instead dropped flowers on the waves;
One could be gracious in the early days.

We speak no more of the Decisive Battle;
If ever there was a Decisive Battle
It is on the deck of an American ship.

Hellcats and Avengers coming on,
Bombers at all points of the clock,
We are fueled for one way only.

Pagoda masts as visible as Fuji,
Two hundred and eight star-planes coming on,
Mainmast hit, return fire defective,
No live practice any more.

Five torpedo hits, starboard engine,
Boiler room flooded,
Several hundred seamen trapped,
Caught between cold water,
Boiling water, steam,
List not corrected, wireless room flooded,
Flag and light signals all that's left,
Decks a shambles, cracked and twisted steel,
Coral color from infernal heat,
Big guns inoperable.

Blast in dispensary kills all present,
Doctors and corpsmen as well,
Communications ended from the bridge,

.   .   .   .

Distress flag hoisted, steering room flooded,
Rudder jammed hard left,
List thirty-five degrees.

Final conference of available staff,
Salutes, bows, prolonged silence,
Shaking of hands, singing and tears.

Deck nearly vertical,
Battle flag touching the waves,
Skidding shells kindling explosions,
Yamoto sliding completely under.

Blast, rumble and shock of compartments,
Bursting from air pressure, magazines exploding,
Complement of two thousand sixty-seven men.

No word for *surrender* in our Code,
No word for *retreat*,
Only *Yamoto*.

• Over Many Seas

(Catullus translation)

Past many nations, over many seas,
Brother, I come to do these obsequies,
Come to present you with the final gift
And to your quiet ashes speak bereft;
For fortune has deprived me of your life,
Fortune has brought me to this deepest grief.
These simple offerings which our parents said
It is our trust to lay before the dead,
Brother, I lay before you. Take them, wet
With your own brother's tears. Here we are met
And here for the last time to you I tell
The *Ave Atque Vale!* Hail! Farewell!

• To Lesbia

(Catullus translation)

My Lesbia, let us live and love
And value at a penny's worth
The common leers and libels of
Old men and all their gamy mirth.

Suns may go down and rise again;
For us when once life's sudden light
Has fallen, what sleep comes on us then?
The sleep of one unbroken night.

Kiss me a thousand kisses, sweet,
To these a thousand thousand add,
And all these thousands then repeat
That none may know the sum we've had.

The best way to confuse these fools
Is to keep kissing while they count
Till they no longer know the rules
By which our mouths and bodies—mount!

• The Rape of Philomel

Procne said, it happened at my wedding
On the wedding night in the bedroom
Foul influences presided
Juno was not there
Hymen was not there
Nor the three Graces in the bride-room
But the Furies came
With fire stolen from a funeral
And a screech owl screamed up in the rafters
Over the bride-bed
While Tereus my husband took my body
And the owl splattered us naked
And that same night I conceived my son
Itys, Itys
And for five years was a peaceful wife
A dutiful queen but begged my husband
Tereus I miss my sister
Send me to Philomel or her to me
It makes no difference which
And with my flesh persuaded him
To send me to Athens or her to Thrace
Till finally Tereus sailed to Athens
Over the curling sea in his king's ship
To bring my sister Philomel
To me to see each other and compare.

Philomel said, when the king came
I mean Tereus my sister's king
He grasped my father's hand, hands of two kings,
And stated his errand that I sail back
To visit Procne in her own palace
But when my father called me to enter
Tereus' eyes gloated, I felt undressed
He scanned my clothes and underneath my clothes
He sweated, he sighed, he stared
His eyes glued to my flesh
Men of his country are notorious for that
He talked too fast, his words foamed
His lips boiled, his eyes wetted
Yet he seemed kind and reverent and soft
I begged my father let me go
O let me go with Tereus to my dear
Which my good father nodded at with frowns
And sob-shaken saw us aboard.

Tereus said, it was a common errand
Though generous for me
To fetch my sister-in-law to see my queen
A visit of alliance, courtesy

.   .   .   .

73

And so I sailed the curling sea to Athens
Pleaded with Pandion the king
To hand his daughter Philomel
Into my trust to bear her to her flesh
Her flesh-and-blood her sister, my queen
And he acceded but when she entered
My blood took fire my insides roiled
Like animals let loose I lost my footing
My brain was like a barn-fire
I thought I'd bribe her nurses have her now
Offer her the richest whore's gold
Or rape her in her room and if I die
What difference does it make, somehow I spoke
The right words and got her to the ship
Shook hands and embraced the king
Who wept to see her go as well he might.

Philomel said, why on his ship
Did Tereus' eyes dog me like a thief
Silkily following my every move
Or now like an eagle gazing down
As if I were a rabbit to be snatched
By ripping claws borne to his crag.

Tereus said, the swift ship finally
Has struck the shore of Thrace, I have her bound
And wrenched to the hut in the black wood
Hurl her down and rip her dress to threads
And mount her like a whore
The more she cries for Procne or her father
Riper more frantic grows my lust
And now she prays and quakes like a lamb
Torn by a wolf or bloodied like a dove
Maimed by a hawk, she tears her hair
Claws at her arms and shrieks her hate
And swears revenge for Procne for herself
Her father for broken vows, for fate
She shall be sworn to all the gods
Till rocks shed tears and stones repeat
The rape of Philomel, till in my rage
I yanked her tongue forth with a pincers
And with my dagger cut it off
Where it lay throbbing at her feet as if
To creep back to its mistress, foul thing
Twitching like a serpent's tail, and watching
I mounted her again and gorged my pleasure.

Procne said, my sister fell asleep
On board Tereus' ship and a tall wave
As if for love of her in all her beauty
Curled over her and took her in its arms
And bore her down to bottomless sleep,
Tereus told me this with howling moans
And is disconsolate and hunts each day
In the dark wood to control his sorrow,
As for me I dress in black
And go to see the sepulchre I built
To pray and do the rites of my dear dead
Sister Philomel.

Philomel thought, I will pick out old threads
And weave my story in the frame
For Procne's eyes to read
The old servant will take it to the queen
A present from an unknown hand.

Procne said, when I unwound the gift
And read the poison of the truth
I locked myself in a far room and wept
Plotted our revenge and held my tongue

.   .   .   .

But on the feast of Bacchus when the night
Shakes with clash of brass and women's shrieks
Rip through the sky and animals are caught
And torn apart and eaten and perhaps
Even a child is caught and torn and eaten
I dressed as Frenzy with the Thracian women
Vines in my hair the deerskin on my back
Spear at my shoulder, mad with grief
I raced the forest to her cottage
And screaming Bacchus Bacchus smashed the door
And dressed by Philomel as a Bacchante
All draped with ivy and ripe vines
And brought her in terror to the palace
Hid her in a farthest room to weep
In one another's arms and plot the end
How? to burn the palace down
And Tereus in its ruins, use the sword?
Torture his body, stick out his eyes,
Hack him to pieces, cut off his genitals
That have raped all of us and Thrace?
At which my sole son Itys wandered by
Itys the image of Tereus, Itys
His heir, I hugged him close and kissed him

.   .   .   .

Merely my child, a prince, a monster's child
Then Philomel took down a sword for me
I stabbed him through the breast
And my crazed sister seized the sword
And stabbed him through the throat, the room ran blood,
We cut and pared the boy and threw the gobbets
Into the cooking pots and boiled the meat
Itys' hacked head staring from the table.

Tereus said, it is my privilege
This black night of the orgies to be served
Alone upon my throne by my good queen
Who this night is my sole servant
And eat whatever food she sets at table
And after eating to admit my son
Who someday will repeat the privilege,
Bring Itys here.

Procne said, you have your Itys here
Inside you, flesh of your flesh
It is your son you ate for privilege
Monster tyrant rapist
Now you have feasted on your flesh and blood,

.   .   .   .

At which with foaming lips and splashed with gore
Philomel leapt before the king and flung
The dripping boy's head at his father's head
Whose face a map of horror staggered up
And tried to vomit but pulled out his sword.

Fly Philomel I screamed and both of us
Flew down the hallways, suddenly on wings
For Philomel was a nightingale
And I a swallow slicing through the air
And King Tereus with a helmet's crest
And bill shaped like a spear
Leapt in the air to follow us.

The feathers of these birds are stained with murder.

About the Author

KARL SHAPIRO was born in Baltimore, Maryland, and attended the University of Virginia and Johns Hopkins University. In 1946 he was appointed Consultant in Poetry at the Library of Congress, and then, in 1947, he joined the faculty of Johns Hopkins University, where he taught writing courses. From 1950 to 1956 he was editor of *Poetry A Magazine of Verse.* He was professor of English and editor of *The Prairie Schooner* at the University of Nebraska from 1956 to 1966, and professor of English at the Chicago Circle Campus of the University of Illinois from 1966 to 1968. He is now professor of English at the University of California at Davis. He is a member of the National Institute of Arts and Letters. His second volume of verse, *V-Letter and Other Poems,* was awarded the Pulitzer Prize in 1945. He was awarded the Bollingen Prize in Poetry in 1969.

DATE DUE